Treasure Hunters

Written by Philippa Werry
Illustrated by Rob Lang

CHARACTERS

Lexi (alien)

Bik (alien)

Jax (alien)

Fred (security guard)

Fran (security guard)

Ali (alien)

Fred:	Hey, lady! You can't park that... that **contraption** there! Read the signs, why don't you?
Ali:	Excuse me, you foolish Earthling. I am no lady and this fine piece of **technology** is not a contraption. It is, in fact, the very latest model space-bus.
Fred:	That's very **enthralling**, but I'm not at all concerned with what model of bus it is. This is not a parking space.
Bik:	Jax, look up "par king space" in the dictionary.
Jax:	I'm currently investigating, Bik, but you'll be required to exercise some patience. I can't find "par king space" in this ridiculous manuscript of yours.
Lexi:	We are not at all concerned about your "par king space," Earthling.

Fred: But… but… oh, just you wait until I get my **colleague**, the other security guard, over here! She's not going to tolerate your **shenanigans**. Fran will straighten you out!

Ali: Earthling, do be silent for just a moment, please. I need to determine whether the Treasure Indicating Machine has sensed any riches.

Lexi: I'll turn it on and see. No, it's not beeping yet.

Bik: It will soon. I'm looking at our flight plan We should be just off the main road.

Lexi: Yes, yes, I know that was our plan, but...

Jax: Don't tell me we disembarked in the wron place again! I was absolutely certain that we should have turned left, not right, at that last **supernova**. But does anybody ever pay attention to what I say?

Lexi: Oh sure, it's always my fault.

Bik: What do those symbols over there say?

Ali: Well, obviously they don't say anything. Oh, you mean you intend me to read thos squiggly little symbols. I believe that they **signify** "Shopping Mall".

Jax: Fine, I guess this will have to do for us, bu we still should have turned...

Fred: Look, there they are! Hey! You! Why haven't you moved that over-sized bus of yours yet? Don't you realise that you're causing a major traffic jam?

Ali: Oh, he's back again, still directing offensi language at us. Jax, look up "jam" in your book of big words.

Jax: "Jam: fruit boiled with sugar." Well, that definition is **preposterous**. We didn't bring any fruit with us, even though I requested some.

Fran: All right, all right. What's all the **commotion** about? First of all, what on earth do you call that weird-looking vehicle? And where did you come from?

Ali: I already explained to your Earthling colleague – it is a space-bus. We come from a far-off place.

Fred: Afaroff Place? Well, I've never heard of it. It must be overseas. Fran, have you ever heard of a foreign city called Afaroff Place?

Fran:	No, Fred, I can't say I have. No matter where it comes from, this bus needs to be moved.
Fred:	I believe we're obliged to report this incident to the command centre. And we would be well advised to keep an eye on this group.
Jax:	Come on, fellow travellers. Enough of this, let's continue with our mission.
Lexi:	Where do you think we'll find the treasure?
Bik:	We can start with this place. J-E-W-E-L-L-E-R-Y.
Ali:	No, no, this **paraphernalia** doesn't look right. They're the wrong shape – and they're too shiny.
Lexi:	What about that enormous building, that one over there: B-A-N-K. Jax, look up "bank" in the book.

Jax: "Bank: the ground on the side of a river or stream." Okay, this just proves that the book isn't helping us. All the little rectangular papers those people are holding would get sodden and **pulpy** in a place like that.

Lexi: Hey, the Treasure Indicating Machine is beeping!

Ali: Quick, lock in the **coordinates**. Where is it pointing?

Lexi: Over there.

Bik: Hurry! Follow the beeping!

Fran: Look at them, they're making no attempt to move that bus of theirs.

Fred: Look! I think we've been more than patient with you. I'm now informing you that if you don't move this bus, we're going to have it towed away!

Ali: And this is the last time I'm going to inform you, it's a space-bus. What is it with the memory span of Earthlings? Now, what is "tow"? Jax, look it up in the book of big words! Fast!

Jax: "Toe: one of the five units at the end of the foot." Why are you making me research such nonsense, Ali?

Bik: Oh, please don't kick our space-bus. We have treasure to find.

Lexi: Finally! Here's some treasure! The machine is beeping like crazy right here. It's pointing at this shop.

Ali: Ah, Lexi, can you smell it? The sweet aroma, the amazing, delicious odour of... treasure.

Bik: Let's go in.

Fred: Didn't you understand what I just said to you? Get back here and move this bus – **pronto**!

Fran: All right – you refused to follow orders, and you just used up your last chance! I'm calling the tow truck!

Lexi: Just look at all these different kinds. Some are dark and some are light.

Jax: There are some with nuts, or peppermint, or cherries. How are we supposed to decide?

Ali: These are worth an absolute fortune.

Bik: I've never seen so much treasure. Look! There are little ones, too.

Jax: I told you we should have brought the bigger space-bus, Lexi. Didn't I say that?

Lexi: Oh sure, it's always my fault.

Fran: They went into the sweet shop, Fred. Quick, we'd better see what they're up to.

Ali: Wait, where is the governor of this fantastic treasure house?

Fred: Treasure house? What are you talking about? This is just a plain old sweet shop.

Bik: Just a sweet shop? There is more treasure here than we have ever seen before!

Fred: Well, it can just stay here while you move your bus!

Jax: Earthling, tell me. What do you call this magnificent treasure?

Fred: Treasure? Do you mean the chocolate? It's called chocolate, not treasure. Gee! What planet are you from?

Ali: Choc-o-late? That is what you call it? We wish to acquire all of it.

Fran: Acquire all of it? Well, I suppose that once you've acquired it, you might finally move your bus – but how *are* you going to pay for it?

Jax: Bik, give me the gold. There, Earthling. This should cover it.

Fred: But... where in the world did they acquire all that gold?

Fran: Just let them pay, Earthling... oops, I mean Fred. Then they'll take their chocolate and move their bus.

Lexi: Come on! We need to get back on the space-bus immediately!

Bik: There. Now all the treasure is in the space-bus. We'll return soon for more!

Fred: Hey, don't let them get away! I haven't even given them a ticket yet for all the trouble they caused.

Fran: It's too late. Look! There they go, straight up into the air!